Modern Curriculum Press
BEGINNING
TO
READ
Series

It's Circus Time, Dear Dragon

Margaret Hillert

Illustrated by David Helton

MODERN CURRICULUM PRESS
Cleveland • Toronto

© **1985 MODERN CURRICULUM PRESS, INC.**
13900 Prospect Road, Cleveland, Ohio 44136.

Softcover edition published simultaneously in Canada by
Globe/Modern Curriculum Press, Toronto.

Library of Congress Cataloging in Publication Data

Hillert, Margaret.
    It's circus time, dear dragon.

    Summary: A boy and his dragon go to the circus where the
dragon performs some unexpected tricks on a high wire.
    (1. Dragons — Fiction.   2. Circus — Fiction)
I. Helton, David, ill.   II. Title.
PZ7.H558Is   1984   (E)   83-22070

ISBN 0-8136-5632-X Paperback
ISBN 0-8136-5132-8 Hardbound

    12 13 14 15 16 17 18 19 20   02 01 00 99 98

I see it. I see it.
Oh, run, run, run.
This is something we will like.

Look at that.
Look up, up, up.
That is pretty.

And here come the funny ones.
Big and little funny ones.
Look here.
Look, look, look.

Now look in here.
Oh, my. Oh, my.
What is in here?

9

10

I see something big.
Big, big, big.
But I do not see you.
Where are you?

11

Oh, no!
What do I see now?
Come here. Come here.
You can not do that.

Come with me.
How funny you are!
But you can't do that.

Now we have to go in here.
This is where it is.
Come on in here.

This is a good spot for us.
Look what we can see.
What a good spot this is.

Oh, no!
How did you get way up there?
That is not a good spot for you.
Come down. Come down.
I did not come here to
see you do something.
I want you here with me.

Now what is this?
What do I see?
What are you on?
Get down. Get down.

You are good at that.
Yes, you are pretty good.
But I want you here.
Come here now.

Not there. Not there.

Do not do that.

I want you to come here to me.

20

Oh, oh.
Look at you.
Look what you have on.
You are so funny.

21

22

And now look at you.
See what you can do.
You can help this big
one jump.
My, what a jump!

But we have to go now.
Mother and Father want us.
Come on.
We have to go.

TICKETS

CIRCUS TODAY

Here is something pretty.
I want a red one.
You can have one, too.

Mother! Father!
Look at us.
See what we have.

Yes, yes.
We see. We see.
What fun for you.

Here you are with me.
And here I am with you.
Oh, what a happy day, dear dragon.

Margaret Hillert, author and poet, has written many books for young readers. She is a former first-grade teacher and lives in Birmingham, Michigan.

It's Circus Time, Dear Dragon uses the 65 words listed below.

a	funny	me	this
am		my	to
and	get		too
are	go	no	
at	good	not	up
		now	us
big	happy		
but	have	oh	want
	help	on	way
can	here	one	we
can't	how		what
come		pretty	where
	I		will
dear	in	red	with
day	is	run	
did	it		yes
do		see	you
down	jump	something	
dragon		spot	
	like		
for	little	that	
fun	look	there	